M^c D O N N E L L

MUTTS

NO. EIGHT

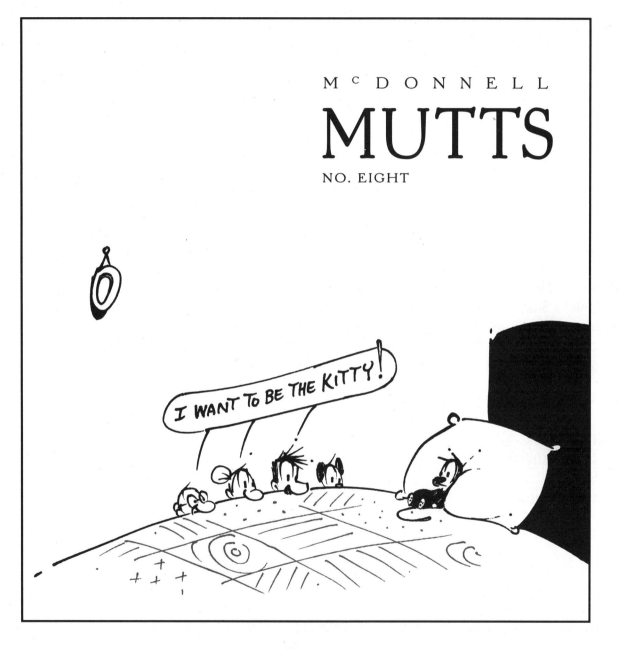

**Andrews McMeel
Publishing**

Kansas City

Other Books by Patrick McDonnell

Mutts
Cats and Dogs: Mutts II
More Shtuff: Mutts III
Yesh!: Mutts IV
Our Mutts: Five
A Little Look-See: Mutts VI
What Now: Mutts VII

Mutts Sundays
Sunday Mornings

The Mutts Little Big Book

Mutts is distributed internationally by King Features Syndicate, Inc. For information write King Features Syndicate, Inc., 888 Seventh Avenue, New York, New York 10019.

05 06 07 BBG 10 9 8 7 6 5 4 3

ISBN-13: 978-0-7407-3305-5
ISBN-10: 0-7407-3305-2

Library of Congress Control Number: 2002113730

I Want to Be the Kitty is printed on recycled paper.

Mutts can now be found on the Internet at
www.muttscomics.com.

ATTENTION: SCHOOLS AND BUSINESSES

Andrews McMeel books are available at quantity discounts with bulk purchase for educational, business, or sales promotional use. For information, please write to: Special Sales Department, Andrews McMeel Publishing, 4520 Main Street, Kansas City, Missouri 64111.

6

8

18

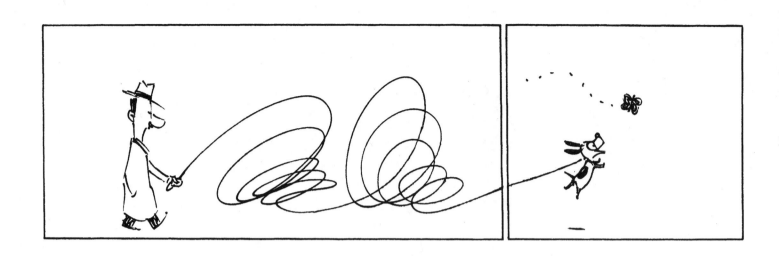

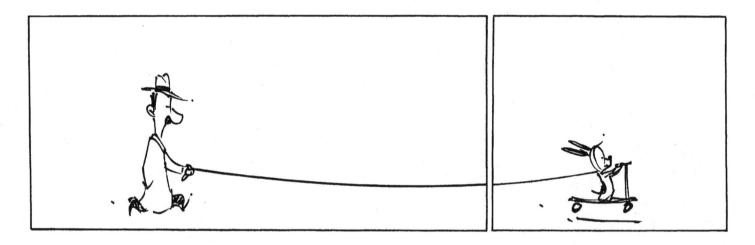

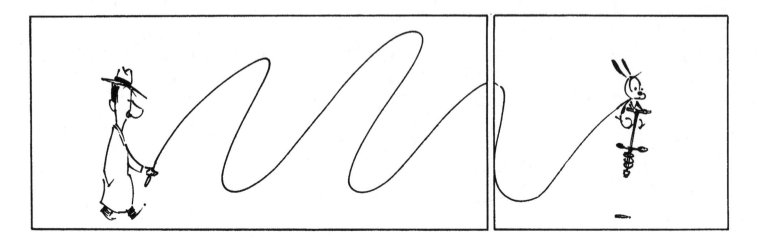

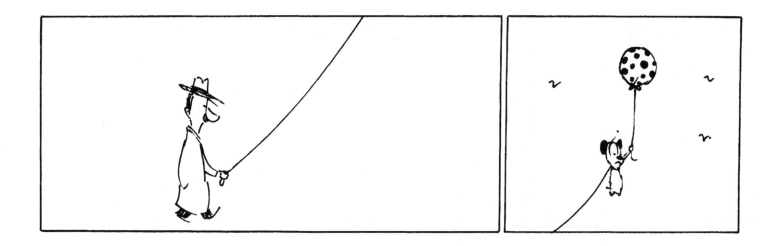

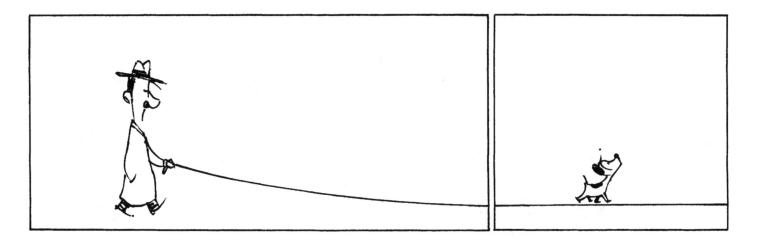

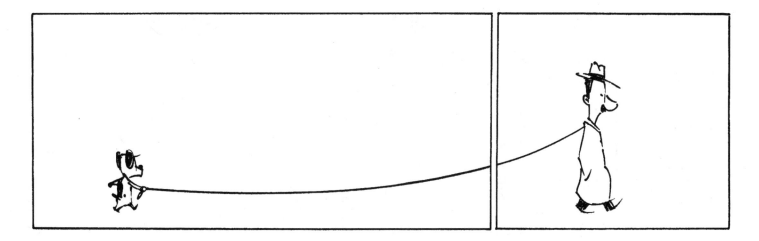

22

MUTTS

30

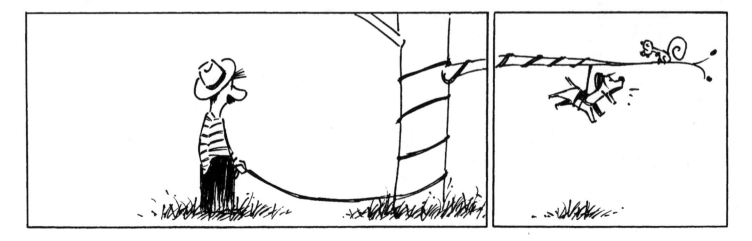

40

42

Mutts!

49

50

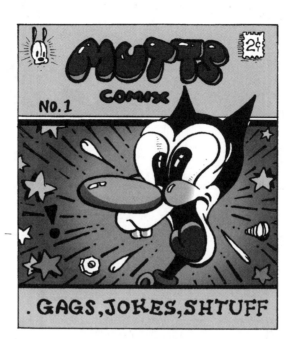

57

MUTTS

YOUR TAIL HAS A **KNOT** IN IT...

SO IT HAS.

HOW!?!

I DUNNO..

IT HAPPENED BEHIND MY BACK.

HEY, CHIPPY! LONG TIME — NO SHEE. WHERE'VE YOU BEEN?

WELL, MOOCH, I RECENTLY HAD THE OPPORTUNITY TO SPEND SOME TIME UNDER YOUR NEXT-DOOR NEIGHBOR'S GARBAGE SHED.

NICE?

OH, YES... TRAVEL BROADENS A PERSON.

THERE'S NEVER A BELLY RUB WHEN YOU REALLY NEED ONE.

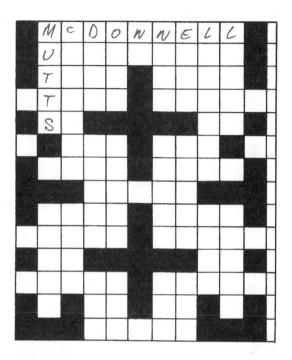

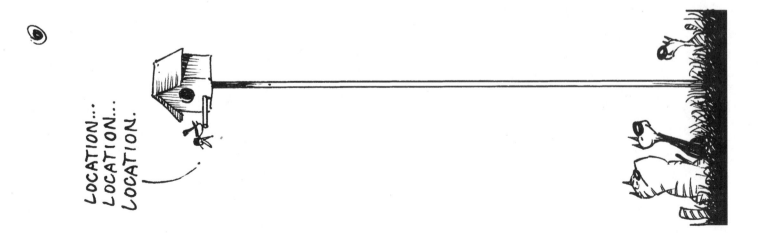

EARL, I'M GOING TO CURE YOU OF **ALL** YOUR BAD HABITS BY SHMACKING AROUND THIS NEWSPAPER !!!

SMACK SMACK SMACK

HA!

NEXT TIME I WON'T USE THE SHUNDAY FUNNIES.

EARL, BY SHMACKING AROUND THIS NEWSPAPER I'LL CURE YOU OF **ALL** YOUR **BAD** HABITS.

SMACK SMACK SMAC

BUT, MOOCH, I DON'T HAVE ANY **BAD** HABITS

CANCEL MY SHUBSCRIPTION

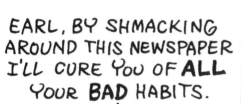

SMACK SMACK SMACK

83

91

Mutts

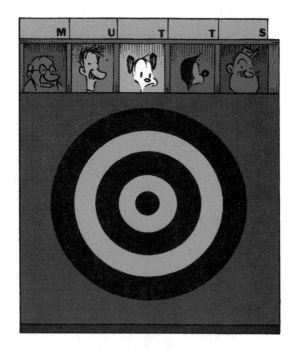

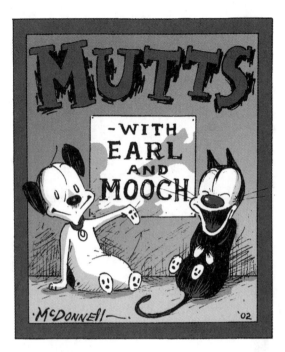

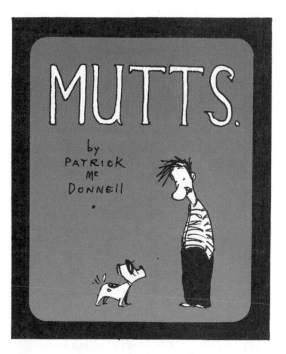

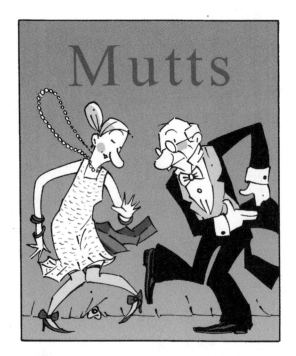